CCSS Genre Tall Tale

Essential Question
What kinds of stories do we tell?
Why do we tell them?

PAUL BUNYAN

BY MAY KENNEDY
ILLUSTRATED BY ALVARO FERNANDEZ VILLA

Chapter 1
The Giant Baby 2

Chapter 2
A World of Blue 6

Chapter 3
The Giant Lumberjack 10

Respond to Reading 16

PAIRED READ One Grain of Rice 17

Focus on Genre 20

CHAPTER 1
THE GIANT BABY

Long ago in Maine, a giant baby boy was born. When he was only two weeks old, he was as large as an adult and had a big, bushy beard!

The baby's name was Paul Bunyan. He grew and grew. When he was nine months old, he was 10 feet tall! He wore the clothes of an **extremely**, or very, large man. He had huge leather boots.

When baby Paul started to crawl, it felt like an earthquake. The ground shook, houses wobbled, and trees rocked from side to side.

The shaking ground frightened the townsfolk, and the shaking hardly ever stopped. Baby Paul Bunyan liked to explore the world around him. That's what babies do!

The unhappy townsfolk told Paul Bunyan's parents to do something about their baby. Filled with sadness, his parents placed him in a huge, floating cradle. They pushed the cradle off the coast of Maine. His mother cried as she waved good-bye to her boy.

However, things soon got worse! When baby Paul turned in his cradle, he made huge waves, which flooded the towns. Then the waves washed the cradle back to shore.

So Paul Bunyan's parents took baby Paul into the woods. They found a cave for him to live in. They didn't want to leave their son, but they had no choice.

Before they left, Paul Bunyan's father gave his son some tools to help him survive. He gave baby Paul a knife, an ax, a fishing pole, and some flint rocks. Then Paul's parents left him there alone.

Baby Paul cried and cried. He cried so much that his tears formed a river.

One day as he cried into the river, Paul heard a splash. It was a fish! Paul grabbed his fishing pole and caught the fish. Then he cleaned the fish with his knife. He chopped firewood with his ax and started a fire with the flint rocks. Soon Paul was eating a delicious meal and his heavy heart felt lighter.

STOP AND CHECK

Why did Paul Bunyan's parents leave him in the woods?

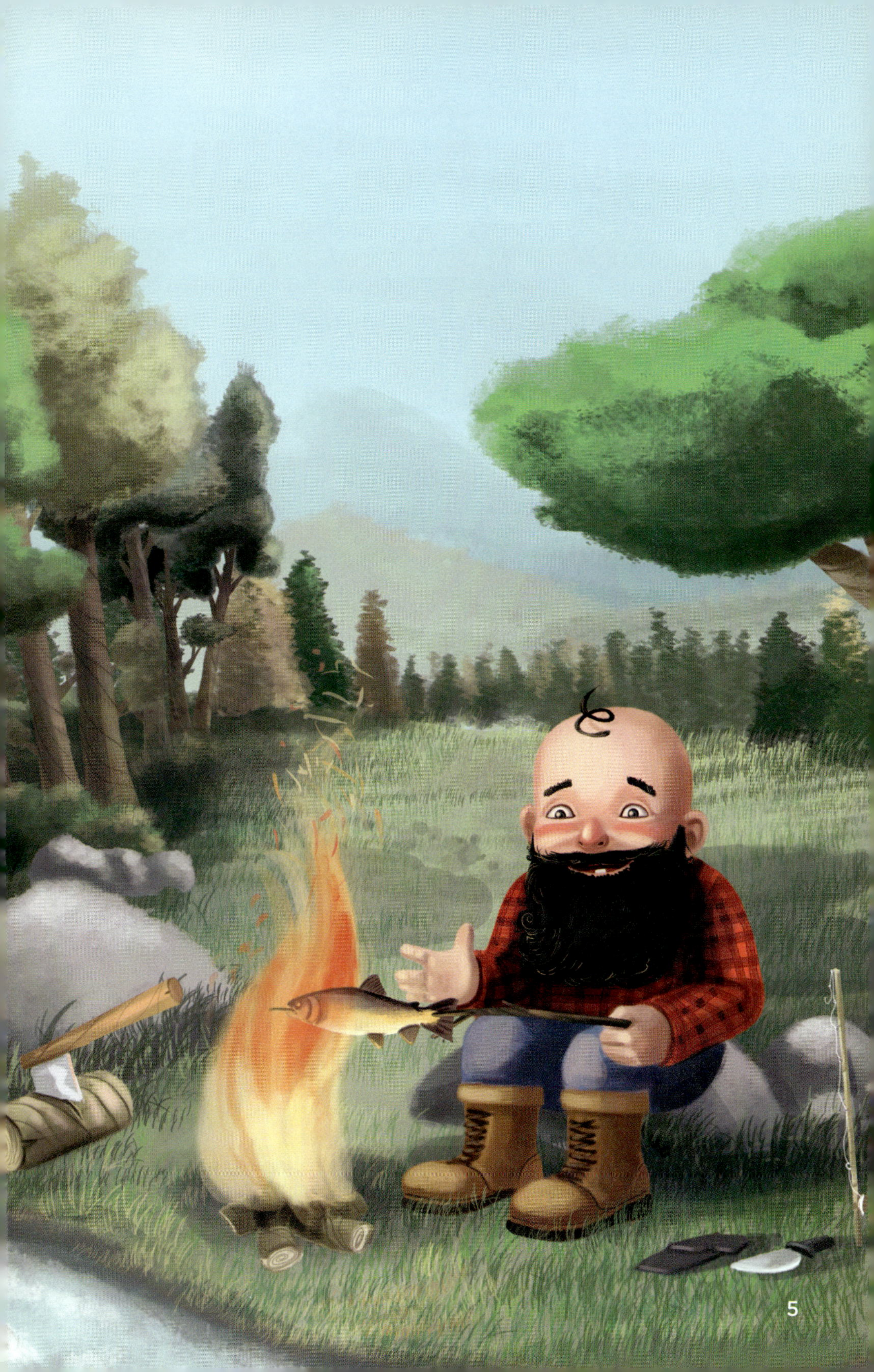

CHAPTER 2
A WORLD OF BLUE

Now Paul Bunyan knew that he could take care of himself. He could get food by fishing. He could make fires to cook and keep warm.

Paul lived alone for 20 years. He had to be brave because the seasons were harsh. The winters had snowstorms and blizzards. There were floods in the spring. The summers had thunderstorms and forest fires. The fall brought wild winds.

STOP AND CHECK

Why did Paul have to be brave?

One cold and wintery day, Paul Bunyan's life changed forever. Big **gusts** of snow blew into his cave, but the snow was not white. It was blue!

Paul peered out of his cave and looked around. He saw blue snow everywhere. It covered the trees and land in every direction.

Paul exclaimed, "It's absolutely beautiful!"

Paul Bunyan was **curious**. What had made the snow blue? He wanted to find out. So Paul dressed in warm clothes and boots. Then he **sauntered** out of his cave and across the blue land. Lightning zapped and thunder clapped in the sky above him.

The wind and the thunder were very loud. They nearly drowned out a faint sound.

"Maa! Maa!"

Paul Bunyan looked around. What was making that noise? Just then he saw a tail poking out of the blue snow.

He pulled and pulled on the tail until out popped a baby ox. It was the biggest baby ox on Earth—and that's no **exaggeration**! The baby ox was blue like the snow.

Paul Bunyan gently picked up the baby ox and carried it back to his cave.

He carefully placed the ox near the fire so the frozen ox would **thaw**. The ox was frightened. "Don't worry, you'll be safe here," said Paul. The baby ox curled up by the fire. It looked perfect there, like a sleeping child **posed** for a painting.

At last Paul Bunyan had a friend. He named his friend Babe the Blue Ox.

Babe grew very quickly. Soon he was as tall as 42 ax handles.

Babe's hunger and thirst grew as fast as he did, but there wasn't a watering hole with enough water for him. So Paul Bunyan dug huge ponds in the ground. Today we call Babe's watering holes the Great Lakes.

STOP AND CHECK

How did Paul Bunyan find his new friend?

CHAPTER 3
THE GIANT LUMBERJACK

Paul Bunyan and Babe enjoyed walking in the woods, among the trees. However, Paul knew that people needed the wood from trees to build houses and barns. He picked up his ax and gave it a swing. One after another, trees crashed down.

Paul Bunyan told Babe, "We must get this lumber to a sawmill."

The closest sawmill was beside a river in Minnesota. Paul and Babe **commenced** their journey to the mill. It didn't take them long. The two giants took **enormous** steps as they walked.

While they were walking, Paul Bunyan saw a river. He thought the logs would travel faster on water, but the river had too many twists and turns. The logs would jam, or get stuck, along the way.

STOP AND CHECK

Why couldn't Paul float the logs down the river?

Paul Bunyan decided to make the river straight. He tied ropes to Babe's harness. Then he tied the ends of the rope to the other side of the river.

"Pull!" he yelled.

Babe pulled. Soon the river was as straight as a tree trunk. Now the two friends could float logs down the river to the sawmill.

Floating logs down the river was hard work. Each day Paul had to **wring**, or squeeze, the sweat out his clothes. A waterfall of sweat fell to the ground.

One night Paul Bunyan told Babe, "We need help. Let's start a logging camp and get loggers to come and work for us."

Paul made signs asking for workers for the logging camp. Many people saw the signs and applied for jobs. However, Paul Bunyan had a special **requirement**. The workers must be more than 10 feet tall! Amazingly, more than a thousand workers met the requirement.

Paul Bunyan built a logging camp for his workers. The bunkhouses were a mile long. The dining tables were enormous, too.

There was one problem. The cook couldn't make enough food for the hungry workers. So Paul Bunyan built a griddle the size of an ice rink! Then he lit a forest fire to heat it.

"How will I grease this huge pan?" the camp cook cried.

Once again, Paul knew what to do. He had a hundred men tie bacon fat to their shoes. Then they skated around the pan to grease it.

STOP AND CHECK

How did Paul Bunyan solve the cook's problems?

Every day Paul Bunyan solved problems. When the workers got frostbite, he told them to grow their beards. The men grew their beards long, then knitted their beards into socks!

Long ago, Paul Bunyan started out alone in a cave. Now he ran a logging camp filled with workers. Yet Paul Bunyan never tried to **impress** anyone, or show off his success. Instead, he and his **faithful**, true friend Babe stuck together and helped many people.

For many years, the workers told stories about **heroic** Paul Bunyan, who was always solving problems. They talked about the good **deeds** he did for others.

The workers also told the story of Paul Bunyan's journey through Arizona. As he walked, he dragged an ax behind him, making a large ditch. Today we call that ditch the Grand Canyon.

Paul Bunyan and Babe loved the outdoors. They were last seen walking to the Arctic Circle. It seems like a strange place for an ox and a lumberjack to go, because there are no trees in that icy land. Maybe Paul Bunyan and Babe just wanted to travel far and explore a new **frontier**, a land where no one had settled.

> **STOP AND CHECK**
>
> How did Paul Bunyan make the Grand Canyon?

Respond to Reading

Summarize

Summarize *Paul Bunyan*. Use important details from the story. Your graphic organizer may help you.

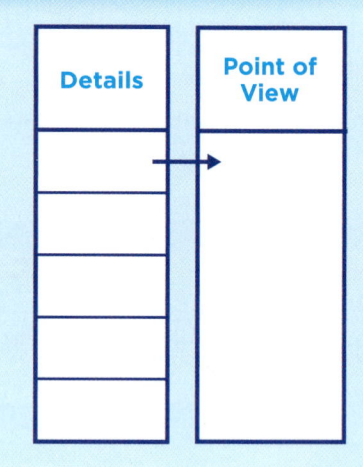

Details	Point of View

Text Evidence

1. What is the narrator's opinion of Paul Bunyan? Give an example of a description that shows this. **POINT OF VIEW**

2. Look at the word *peered* on page 7. Use clues from the paragraph to help you figure out its meaning. **VOCABULARY**

3. Write about how Paul Bunyan feels about Babe. How can you tell? **WRITE ABOUT READING**

Genre > Legend

Compare Texts
Read a legend about a very clever girl.

One Grain of Rice

Long ago in India, there lived a *raja*, or ruler. This raja told all the rice farmers in the land to give him most of the rice they grew. He wanted to save the rice so he would always have something to eat. Soon he had rooms filled with bags of rice.

Then one year, the rice crops did not grow. The people were extremely hungry. They didn't have any food, but the raja would not give them any rice. He said, "I must keep it for myself."

The people grew hungrier, but the raja didn't care. One day, he held a feast in his palace.

A servant and an elephant were sent to get some of his rice. As the elephant returned to the palace, grains of rice fell from the baskets it was carrying on its back. A girl named Rani ran beside the elephant and caught the rice with her skirt.

"Stop! Thief!" cried a guard.

Rani thought quickly. "I'm collecting the rice to give back to the raja," she said.

The raja heard what happened and decided to give Rani a reward. Clever Rani asked him for one grain of rice.

"One grain of rice?" cried the raja. "Let me give you a better reward than that."

"All right," said Rani. "Give me one grain of rice today. Then, the next day give me double the number of grains you gave me the day before. Do this for 30 days."

The raja liked Rani's request. He handed Rani one grain of rice.

On the second day, Rani received two grains of rice. On the third day, she received four grains. On the thirteenth day, she received 4,096 grains of rice. By the thirtieth day, Rani needed hundreds of elephants to carry all of her rice. One grain of rice quickly became more than one billion grains of rice! This happened through a process called doubling.

"Now I have no rice!" cried the raja. "What will I do?"

Rani gave almost all of her rice to the hungry people, but she kept one basket of rice for the raja. Before Rani gave it to him, she asked him to never take more than he needed again. Of course, he said yes.

Make Connections

Why do you think people continue to share the legend *One Grain of Rice*? ESSENTIAL QUESTION

How are Paul Bunyan and Rani similar? How are they different? TEXT TO TEXT

Focus on Genre

Tall Tales Tall tales are stories about heroes who can do amazing things. They include events that could not happen in real life. The characters and their actions are exaggerated. Exaggeration makes characters seem bigger, better, or more important than they really are. For example, when baby Paul was left in the woods, "He cried so much that his tears formed a river."

Read and Find Exaggeration is often used to describe Paul Bunyan. Turn to page 2. Find an exaggeration in the last paragraph. What makes it exaggerated?

Your Turn

Work with a partner. Tell why these actions are exaggerated.

"Paul Bunyan built a griddle the size of an ice rink!"

"He lit a forest fire to heat it."

"The men skated around the pan to grease it."